For some an end,
but really a beginning.
Hmmm?

THE PRINCIPAL STRIKES BACK

Jarrett J. Krosoczka

Scholastic Inc.

For Max, Tate, and Finn

Scholastic Children's Books,
Euston House, 24 Eversholt Street,
London NW1 1DB, UK

A division of Scholastic Ltd
London ~ New York ~ Toronto ~ Sydney ~ Auckland
Mexico City ~ New Delhi ~ Hong Kong

First published in the US by Scholastic Inc, 2018
First published in the UK by Scholastic Ltd, 2018
This edition published by Scholastic Ltd, 2019

ISBN 978 1407 19246 8

A CIP catalogue record for this book is available from the British Library.

P̶rinted by CPI Group (UK) Ltd, Croydon, CR0 4YY
Papers used by Schola̶ ... are made from wood grown in sustaina̶ble forests.

This is a wor̶ ... of fiction. Names, characters, places, incidents and dialo̶
are products of t̶ ... are used fictitiously, any resembl̶e to
actual pe̶ ... s or locals is entirely coincidental.

A long time ago in a galaxy far, far away. . . .

Victor Starspeeder has journeyed day and night, battling and defeating evil droids along the way. He is nearly at his destination—the very pinnacle of the mountain! It has been a journey of self-discovery and triumph over adversity. But there is just one last obstacle in his way—the last year of school! This Jedi Master reaches for his lightsaber and lights up the night sky.

7

Hexaday

I have no idea how I am going to face everyone back at school. I know that all of the kids have been talking about me behind my back. I mean, I see what they've been posting to Stargram! Lots of shady comments coming from some of my classmates. I'd like to think if the tables were turned, I'd be more understanding, but I dunno. A Sith came to our school because of me. My dad, the one that I thought died a hero's death, turned out not to be dead and to be a total Sith. Awkward, right? And sure, I helped defeat him along with my friends, but I can't blame them for being a bit mad at me. I mean, had I stayed at my old school, nobody at the Coruscant campus would have to have dealt with it. And even though my sister, Christina, was working with Yoda to bring Pops to justice, she took a hit from kids who thought she was a Sith herself. So, there's like this cloud hanging over my head.

There are some people who still blame me for getting Zachary O'Halleran expelled. Even when that dude was a total creep and headed to the dark side himself, everyone knew good ol' Zach as this fun-loving popular kid.

O'Halleran Expelled

Look, I mess up sometimes, I'll admit it. I don't mean to. But now when I misstep, I'm afraid people are going to think the worst of me. I tried to save the school, and people are treating me like I'm the problem. With Christina graduated and off on her apprenticeship, I'll be stuck at Jedi Academy all on my own—with nobody to look after me. The son of a Sith . . .

I wish I could use the Force to make all of my problems float away . . .

Stargram

Zav-YEAH: Alderaan all day, every day. Can't wait to get back to #JediAcademy!

 12  7

MAYATHEATER: Theater door at WOOKIEE SIDE STORY! #ROAWRRR!

 15 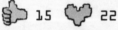 22

ArtemisCC: Too many books, not enough time.

 4 3

Coletastic: last year of Jedi Academy and already my dad can't deal.

 7 11

Elaraforce: Missing my Victor! #Throwback

 8 7

Excuse me, can I ask you a question?

Sure. What's up?

Is it weird to be away at Jedi Academy and separated from your parents?

Nah, that's the best part.

I just ... I just don't know anybody there.

Don't worry, you'll make some great friends.

You sort of build up your own little family away from home.

Cool.

You'll do just fine. Hang in there, man.

Excuse me.

beep beep

Vic, it's me. It is so weird not to be on a school shuttle this time of year, but I am having the most amazing adventures. Even though I'm having so much fun, apprenticeship is hard work. It makes finals seem like an afternoon stroll on Naboo. But it is all so totally worth it.

Anyhow, I need to run. But if I time this right, you'll get this before you see everyone back at Jedi Academy. You're on your own now, kid. But let me tell you this—ignore the haters. There's nothing you can do about them, just keep your head up high.

Was that your mom?

Close. My big sister.

13

The Padawan Observer

SWEEPING CHANGES AT JEDI ACADEMY

It is with great enthusiasm that the Jedi Academy administration announces measures that will keep the student population safe. As reported earlier, a Sith sneaked onto campus at the very end of the last academic year. Many parents voiced outrage over such a development. Principal Mar has brought onto the staff Commander ZC-04. Commander ZC-04 will lead a new group of security droids who will be tasked with patrolling the hallways and perimeter of the school at all hours of the day. All students must be in their bunks by 21:00. There will be absolutely no lenience on this time frame. It is imperative that we secure all students safely in their bunks at the designated time.

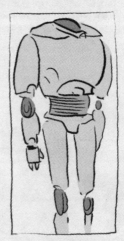

Commander ZC-04

Jedi Academy is getting a fleet of security droids.

COMICS

WOOKIEE CIRCUS

SPOT THE DROIDRENCES!

Rwooooar!"

HUTTFIELD

IT'S THE SIMPLE THINGS IN LIFE THAT MAKE ME HAPPY.

LIKE REVENGE.

YOUNGLINGS

I JUST CAN'T FIND NEW POWER CONVERTERS.

HAVE YOU TRIED TOSCHE STATION, CHABA DOWN?

LIKE I CAN GET TO TOSCHE STATION! I'M DOOMED.

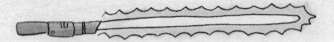

ASK MS. CATARA!

Dear Ms. Catara,

I have a friend who has been a bit distant this summer. I think that maybe he thinks that I will think less of him because he has a parent who was up to some bad things. How do I let my friend know that he is still cool with me?

Sincerely,
A Concerned Friend

Dearza Concerned Friendza,

My, my, my. It sounds a like youz friend is going through some tough times. But youza good friend for wanting to find a wayz to helps. A good friend iza patient and a good friend listens. So, if you get youz friend to opens up, listen and validate theirs feelings, but no need to pass youz own judgments on the situation. Let your friend a know that you are a there, and whens they are ready, they will a talk to you.

XO,
Ms. Catara

GALAXY FEED

5 Famous
Jedi that
Every Padawan
Should Know
Before
Graduation

Life Hacks
that Padawans
Can't Live
Without

LOL! to Get
You through
Your Monoday

Good luck. I'll look for you in the cafeteria.

Thanks!

By the way, what's your name?

Devlon.

Cool. I'm Victor.

You're Victor? As in Victor Starspeeder? Oh.

Uh . . . see ya around!

Hello, Victor.

ARTEMIS! My man, how are you?

Heptaday

These new security droids are going to be a problem. How is me being friends with P-10 going to cause trouble? Never underestimate the bond between a boy and his droid!

Who's a good droid?

And this curfew thing is stupid. A Sith could sneak in during the daytime just as easily as they could during the night. None of it makes sense. Also, how much money did the school just spend on these hunks of junk? Droids ain't cheap! I really, really want to lie low this year and stay out of trouble. I'm going to bite my lip as best I can, but I just can't stand for things being unfair. All of my classmates have to deal with this nonsense because my dumb dad thought I'd be game for heading over to the dark side. There has to be an easier way to keep everything Sith-free without our style being completely cramped.

Attention! Attention! We must get started on our first Drama Club meeting.

Bee-ba bee.

Well, everyone, we have to figure out a way around this curfew.

If we want to put on the best possible show, we need to put the time in for the sets and rehearsal. I make a motion to meet early in the morning before classes start.

No way!

We'll be done before curfew.

That'll never work!

Who wants to wake up at that hour?

We'll start on time this year—promise!

I'm afraid that Ms. Phoenix is correct about the length of rehearsals.

Based on a review of the past ten years of rehearsal records, Padawans went past the scheduled rehearsal end times in 67 percent of the instances.

Beee . . . .

Master Yoda, I will not allow any leniency on the security measures.

No, nor should you. But adjust to the new schedule the Padawans will. Yes? Yes.

Sleep makes for a rested brain, ready to learn. An early rehearsal, work it will not.

But, Master Yoda—

Learn to manage time effectively, young Padawans will. Strong time management skills, a powerful Jedi must master.

We will make the absolute best of it, Master Yoda, I assure you.

I will be watching closely. I am of the mind-set that droids have no place in instructing students on managing their emotions.

Spoke of this we did, Commander ZC-04. Quite the show, T-3PO and RW-22 produce, they do. Stay as it is, Drama Club will.

We appreciate your faith in us, Master Yoda.

Bee ba bee!

Zavyer, did you just hear what I just heard? ZC-04 wants to can T-3PO and RW-22?!

That is so messed up!

Go on, the show will— if you make it so.

Triday

Auditions were yesterday. I gave it my all, more than my all, because I did not want to disappoint T-3PO and RW-22. I don't even care if I get a big role. I just want to be a part of the team and make this last musical count! I always had dreams of getting the lead, but there is no bad part when you are all working as a team to put on the best show possible. And this year, it's the theater kids versus Commander ZC-04. We will prove him wrong. We have the best possible advisers for the Drama Club, and we'll get this show up and running without staying out all night long to make it work. I don't know how I'll get all the sets done and be the lead. I'll really have to skip some sleep!

The Padawan Observer

EDITED BY THE STUDENTS OF JEDI ACADEMY   Vol. MXVII #3

DESPITE SETBACKS, ANNUAL MUSICAL ANNOUNCED

There has been much buzz around campus about the state of the annual musical. With Commander ZC-04's philosophies on droid-human relations, there was a concern that T-3PO and RW-22 would be out as Drama Club moderators. "They would be irreplaceable," said Drama Club president Maya Phoenix. *The Padawan Observer* sent inquiries to other faculty members to gauge interest in running the theatrical group of Padawans, should there be a need for a new faculty leadership. "I'd sooner lose both arms in a lightsaber duel," stated Mr. Zefyr. "Rooooooooaw!" responded Kitmum, which we took to mean that she was not interested. "I am delighted that we have the continued support of Master Yoda," said T-3PO. "And this year, we will be putting on a production of *Grease-Wing Starfighter*."

What do you think about the new security droids?

Artemis:
I'd rather not be interviewed for this.

Tessen:
We're just lucky that there isn't another Sith attack.

Maya:
Their curfew punishes well-behaved Padawans.

Did you guys see that? Those kids were totally talking smack about me.

beep beep

Hey! I just got an alert on my datapad! The cast list has been posted outside the theater door!

Let's go check it out! We can swing by on the way to lunch.

Ugh! You guys are so obsessed with the musical, you're not going to stick up for me?

Wait up, guys, I'll come with you.

Just remember, Victor, every part is important.

Yeah, yeah, I know.

I'm just trying to manage your expectations.

I'm happy to be a supporting player.

Um . . . Vic . . .

Pentaday

I don't know how I got the lead. Maybe the Danu Zaku character doesn't sing much? Or is he supposed to be tone-deaf? I mean, I am handsome like he is, but . . . What I do know about this show is that my character and Maya's character fall in love, and Elara's character tries to get in the way of that and makes Maya's character's life super difficult. If I thought T-3PO and RW-22 were capable of trying to mess with us, I would say that they deliberately set us up to have months of super-awkward rehearsals. I used to like Maya, as in like-like her, but I am so over that. And Elara is sweet and all, and one of my best friends, but I know she crushes on me. I'm thinking I really need to just focus on me right now. And the fact that Elara knows that I used to have a thing for Maya, well—this just got really tricky. Couldn't I have scored a part like Mechanic #2? And I wish that Elara could acknowledge that Maya and Zavyer sort of have a connection going on. I think that we all just need to follow Yoda's advice and avoid these sort of relationships altogether, but it's hard to ignore all these feelings. Middle school. Is. So. COMPLICATED!

Dating leads to jealousy, jealousy leads to contempt, contempt leads to the dark side.

Whoza has time for dating anyhowz? Youza need to focus on youz works!

RAOOOWR!

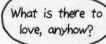

What is there to love, anyhow?

A broken heart does not save the galaxy.

It is important that one is properly seated when entering hyperspace. And safety first means . . .

Always wear your seat harness.

Yes, you don't want to come out of hyperspace flattened against the viewport.

Mr. Starspeeder, am I boring you with this safety protocol?

Huh. No. I'm right here with you, Mr. Zefyr. Hyperspace. Seat harnesses.

35

Later, in Yoda's class . . .

Alone with one's thoughts, a Jedi must often be.

Not easy, but ignore distractions a young Jedi must. Clear your thoughts.

On breathing focus, close the world out and feel the Force that surrounds you.

Good, young Padawans, a handle on this you are gaining.

But amongst you, burdened with thoughts of the past you are. Push the past aside and focus on the future, you must.

To move forward into the future and fully embrace the ways of the Force, this is the only way.

Quadday

Man, the consequences of messing up are huge once you get into the serious Jedi stuff. I have to manage all of these classes and obligations with the musical while sorting out how to balance a starship over my head with my eyes closed? Next thing you know, Yoda will want me to do this upside down while he balances on my feet! Then there's this whole thing about exiting hyperspace wrong and ending up as a space pancake. If I want to command a starship ever, I need to double down on paying attention in Zefyr's class. Never mind dealing with all these kids who look at me sideways in the hallway. They think that I don't notice them whispering about me, but I guess my handle on the Force is better than I realize—because I sense their judgment, and it isn't cool. I'm totally getting blamed for the changes that are sweeping Jedi Academy. I seriously doubt there will be any Sith who dare step foot on Jedi Academy grounds again. And with my father behind bars, he won't be back looking for me anytime soon.

I am way behind on set design. Rehearsals are going okay, but I have no idea how Coleman and Maya memorized all their lines for all of those shows. They always make it seem so effortless. I have to deliver my lines while pretending that I am actually listening to the other actors and not just waiting for them to get through their lines so that I can deliver mine. Yoda tells me that balancing all of this will help me in the future, especially when managing all of the responisbilities of a Jedi.

You wanted to see me, Ms. Catara?

Welcome, welcome, Victor Starspeeder! Pleaza, sit! Sit!

Oh yes. Victor, Iza looked at youz schedule, and youza taking on so many things. Too many things!

I want to make the most of my last year at Jedi Academy.

Sure, but by trying to be good at everything, youza going to fall short on so many things. Weeza need to know our limitations, Victor. Theeza over-scheduling thing iza not goods for your minds.

But I'm doing great!

But are youz, though?

Pentaday

Ms. Catara was right. I am trying to do too much. I can't rehearse for the lead AND design the set AND give my classes my all AND get some good chill time with my friends. Something has to give. As much as I hate to quit it, I'm going to leave set design. Zavyer is a talented artist, and he will do the job justice. But here's the secret—I kinda don't want him to get all the attention for doing a job that I am known for. But I have to make room in my schedule. And I am not about to give up the lead! Sure, this is a team effort, but I am going to be a star!

I'd better start practicing my autograph!

The Padawan Observer

EDITED BY THE STUDENTS OF JEDI ACADEMY   Vol. MXVII #4

STAR PUPIL PLACED ON PROBATION

Artemis Oophanoe is not known for being on the wrong side of the rulebook at Jedi Academy. But the studious Padawan, who has not had a single day of truancy, was found outside his dormitory beyond curfew last night. Oophanoe was discovered leaving the library at 21:15 by Commander ZC-04. Oophanoe refused to comment for this article, but ZC-04 stated, "Let this be a lesson to all students. I will not differentiate between research and rambunctiousness. If you are not in your dormitories by the designated time, you will be punished. Should Oophanoe be found outside of his dormitory past curfew again, he will be expelled from Jedi Academy."

CHEF JETTSTER'S DAILY SPECIALS

Monoday: Porgsicles
Duoday: Slimeballs
Triday: Blue Milkshakes
Quadday: Vegetable Souffle
Pentaday: Taco Party

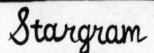

VICT-orious: Total garbage chute!
#FreeArtemis

👍 34 💛 89

Elaraforce: Jedi Academy's
hardest-working Padawan! #FreeArtemis

👍 24 💛 78

MAYATHEATER: Locked away in the dorms
when we could be rehearsing
in the theater.

👍 9 💛 5

Hexaday

Semester break could not have arrived soon enough! I can't wait to get away from that scrap pile ZC-04. He claims to be looking out for students' best interests, but how do you punish a kid like Artemis?! Droid's got himself some issues! Normally, semester break would be all bittersweet because I'd miss my friends, but this year my friends are all coming to Naboo! I can't wait to show them around. We're going to go on hikes, chill out by the lake. It'll be the very best. And my mom won't even freak out if we aren't in our beds by 21:00. The guys will all crash in my room while Maya and Elara will be getting Christina's old room. I only wish that we could smuggle P-10 off of Coruscant!

But don't you prefer the wide-open spaces over the temperature-controlled rooms of Cloud City?

Not really. But the company is good.

Hey! Let's go swimming!

Last one in is a farting eopie!

But the odds of us all getting together like this on a regular basis are statistically unlikely.

Yeah, I don't want to end up like all those old Jedi we saw at the reunion last year. So lame.

Well, let's just savor this moment! All of us together.

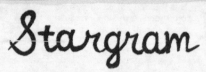

Stargram

Elaraforce: A little piece of paradise. #Naboo

 12  7

ArtemisCC: #Allergies

 15 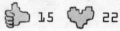 22

MAYATHEATER: Memorizing lines with an amazing view!

👍 4 🤍 3

Coletastic: Love these guys!

👍 7 🤍 11

VICT-orious: Happy trails to the very best! See you all back at school!

👍 8 🤍 7

Pentaday

I wish semester break could have lasted forever. I'd give anything to have my friends with me again, all on my home planet. Although I think Artemis won't be back anytime soon—he really prefers air-conditioning. I can't blame him with his allergies and all, but I'm proud of him for at least trying to do some outdoorsy stuff with us.

Sure, my friends and I all have plenty of the school year left, but I am dreading what is waiting for me when I get back to Jedi Academy. And what is waiting for me is ZC-04—he's going to be all up in my business. Maya warned me not to criticize him on Stargram, but I figured he'd never see it—I had all of my Stargram settings set to private! It's MY Stargram feed after all. What is he? A total creeper? On my way back to Jedi Academy, that new kid was on my shuttle again. I figured I'd make small talk to pass the time. That is, if he wasn't afraid I was a Sith . . .

Hey, Devlen. How's everything going for you at school?

Oh, hey. School is okay. The classes are tough and I'm getting a ton of homework, but I've made some good friends.

Cool. Yeah, the path to becoming a Jedi isn't an easy one. But it'll be so worth it.

Totally.

Who's your favorite teacher?

Mr. Zefyr!

Wha?! For real?

He's a good teacher.

Huh. He's always been pretty mean to me.

Maybe you got on his dark side, um, I mean his bad side!

Huh. Yeah, maybe.

So . . . what's your favorite class?

Droid Mechanics 101.

I never took that elective.

It's fun. I want to build droids someday. I think that'd be a cool job.

56

The Padawan Observer

EDITED BY THE STUDENTS OF JEDI ACADEMY Vol. MXVII #5

MAR OUT, ZC-04 IN—JEDI ACADEMY'S NEW PRINCIPAL

In a shocking reorganization, Jedi Academy's longstanding principal has been removed from his post and will be replaced by the top security droid. While Mar will no longer serve as Jedi Academy's head of school, he will curiously remain on campus serving as an office manager. Commander ZC-04 will be the school's first droid principal. The move was executed by the board of directors in response to the rise of criticism of Mar on social media by both students and parents. "I am delighted to take on this post," said Commander ZC-04. "I look forward to advancing the discipline that I initiated as head of security. These are dangerous times and we just cannot afford to allow for weak leadership."

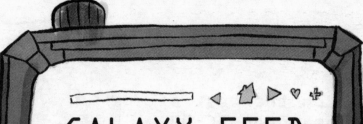

GALAXY FEED

Why Commander ZC-04 Is Jedi Academy's Best Hope
Sponsored Post

- He brings order and discipline.
- He is organized.
- He will keep students safe.
- Upgrades to his central computer will keep him up-to-date.
- He has a history of defeating Sith.
- He has a fantastic cupcake recipe.

From the Desk of
Commander ZC-04

Here is an addendum to the rules
set forth in the Jedi Academy
student handbook:

-Mingling in hallways is not
allowed.

-Students can travel in groups no
larger than two.

-Backpacks are forbidden. Students
must carry all school supplies.

-After curfew, students shall study,
not socialize.

-Any and all field trips are hereby
cancelled forever. No exceptions.

-Droids will be banned from student
activities until reprogramming can
be executed.

WHAT I THINK OF ZC-04 AND HIS NEW RULES.

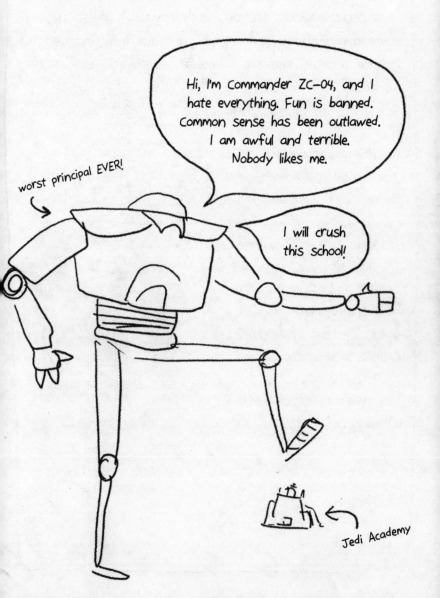

worst principal EVER!

Hi, I'm Commander ZC-04, and I hate everything. Fun is banned. Common sense has been outlawed. I am awful and terrible. Nobody likes me.

I will crush this school!

Jedi Academy

Duoday

Commander ZC-04 has been as unhinged as I imagined he would. Nobody is happy with these new rules and nobody here can figure out how in the galaxy any of this would make us safer. Banning backpacks is ridiculous.

Going on an annual field trip is one of the most treasured traditions at Jedi Academy. I mean, there is only so much you can learn about a planet from a screen. You need to smell its air, set foot on its soil! And we'll see how the annual musical goes. T-3PO and RW-22 aren't allowed to serve as faculty advisers, so now we are stuck with Kitmum.

Living beings aren't always
your best bet when it comes
to drama direction . . .

Rwoooar? Rwoooar!

T-3PO and RW-22, along with P-10, are set to get
reprogrammed, which is so lame. I can't let this happen,
especially to my poor little pal, P-10! These droids have
the best personalities and I don't even want to think
about what ZC-04 would do to them.

Die, Bantha fodder!

BEE BWEE BEWW!

None of my friends want to really talk about it, though.
Everyone is afraid that ZC-04 is listening in on all of
our conversations. But we have to do something to put a
stop to this madness. We just have to!

Oh, and Elara has barely said a word to me since Maya
and I had to rehearse the scene where our characters
kiss. I need to let her know that there were absolutely
no feelings behind that at all!

And that is why a Jedi must never be far from their lightsaber. But remember—a lightsaber, while an elegant and graceful weapon, must only be utilized when all forms of negotiations have failed.

Mr. Starspeeder, is today's lesson boring you?

No, I, uh . . .

To the front of the class, Starspeeder.

Where is your lightsaber, Starspeeder?

It should be right here on my belt... wait. Maybe it's at my desk?

WRONG!

I have it here. You need to be quicker on your feet if you want to succeed as a Jedi.

But—how did you?

The Force, Starspeeder. Maybe you've heard of it?

Starspeeder, I would hate to see you get a failing grade in my classes. I'd hate to see it because that would mean I'd need to deal with you all over again next year.

I'm not going to fail.

Well, my Padawan, I'm afraid you are teetering close to doing just that. Get focused and stay focused. Now, take your seat!

Monoday

At first I thought Mr. Zefyr was joking, but he wasn't playing around. I seriously could fail his classes and then I wouldn't graduate with my friends. Never mind living up to my sister's legacy and what everyone would think of me then, but what Jedi would want to take on an apprentice who had trouble passing classes on lightsabers and starships? But he could be a little less mean about things? He didn't need to embarrass me like that in front of the entire class. I have a lot on my mind! Like, how do I save the droids? Does everyone still think I'm a weirdo because of my dad? Whatever happened to Zefyr when he was a kid to make him so cruel?

I wonder if Zefyr is jealous that ZC-04 is now the toughest faculty member at Jedi Academy? Maybe they have cruel duels in the teachers' lounge?

I thrive off the tears of students.

I thrive off their broken bones.

ZC-04 would definitely be the top creep, but Zefyr has broken more students' spirits over his time here at Jedi Academy.

While I'll miss my friends when I graduate . . . *if* I graduate . . . at the end of the year, I won't miss getting harassed by my teachers. Life is going to be so much easier once I'm done with school. Nobody to tell me where to be and when to be there. I have a big exam coming up in Zefyr's class, and I had better ace it. Sure, staying alive while coming out of hyperspace is important, but so is showing my teacher that I know what's up!

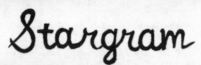

Stargram

VICT-orious: Another boring night in my bunk when we all could be hanging out.

 12  7

ArtemisCC: Getting those apprenticeship applications in.

 15 22

MAYATHEATER: Is there anybody out there who speaks Wookiee that could help us out in Drama Club?

👍 4   💜 3

Coletastic: Trying to enjoy these final months of Jedi Academy, but have SO much work!

👍 7   💜 11

The Padawan Observer

EDITED BY THE STUDENTS OF JEDI ACADEMY Vol. MXVII #6

SEMESTER SOLDIERS ON

Despite restrictions brought on by increased security, life on campus is buzzing. Students seem to really appreciate the extra level of safety. "The new curfew offers me more time to remain in my bunk and accomplish schoolwork," said one student. Commander ZC-04 is very pleased. "Students are adjusting very well to the new regulations set forth at Jedi Academy," he stated. "Despite a few exceptions, the students' behavior has been exemplary."

ASK MS. CATARA!

Dear Ms. Catara,

There is this . . . um . . . friend of mine who won't speak to me. She says that she isn't jealous that I . . . um . . . shook hands with another friend. But that handshake was just for a part we are playing for a . . . class book report. Anyhow, how do I let her know that the handshake was just part of the job and it didn't mean anything emotionally?

Sincerely,
A. Handshake

Dearza A. Handshake,

Wellz, we must always be honest about our feelingz. If youza haven't confronted this directlies with you friends, they really deserve to be heard out. Maybe she suspects there iza something mores to the handshake that you aren't willing to admit? Either wayz, be sensitive to youz friends feelings and let them know that youza wants to shake their hand because youza means it inside your heart.

XO,
Ms. Catara

Quadday

I haven't seen P-10 around, and I will just be gutted if he's already been reprogrammed. None of my friends think it's that big of a deal. But if ZC-04 is willing to rewire the personalities of everyday protocol droids, where will he stop? He's already controlling how early we go to bed and how many people we can hang with in the school hallways. Before you know it, we won't even be allowed to have friends at Jedi Academy!

And the articles in *The Padawan Observer*? Something seems off to me. It's like ZC-04 is writing the articles himself or something. I don't know anybody who is excited about the curfew or any of the new rules.

If none of my friends will help get to the bottom of this and fix it, I'll do so on my own. I at least owe it to everyone, maybe then kids won't look at me sideways in the school hallway. I'll show them that I am a hero, they'll see what Vic is capable of! As soon as this test for Mr. Zefyr is over this afternoon, I am going to do some investigating and do everything I can to get P-10 back. Master Yoda tells us that implementing practical use of the Force is what will help us grow as Jedi. It's time I use everything I've learned so far to help this school that has given me so much.

Did you see that? People stop talking when I walk by. I know they're talking trash!

Don't worry about them, worry about this test. Are you ready for it?

As ready as I'll ever be. You?

I'm hoping I do decently enough.

Where's Mr. Zefyr?

So nice to see you, too, Starspeeder. Now take a seat. Mr. Zefyr's services will no longer be needed at this school.

WHAT?!

You're lucky that I am using a training saber. Otherwise, your hand would be gone!

Who's next?

Sir, I don't see how this will help us navigate hyperspace.

How did I know that Starspeeder would have something to say?

Well, it seems like this is an unnecessary change in course. You were just pretty rough on Artemis—

You Padawans need to toughen up! You don't know what rough is; you don't know the hardships you'll face once you leave Jedi Academy!

80

Triday

Okay, ZC-04 is just plain ca-razy. Also, since when can droids use the Force? Something is not right here. It's like he has a vendetta against students. I mean, sure, I've said that about Mr. Zefyr, but he does end up getting results. And Zefyr was right—I should make sure that I am fully aware of where my lightsaber is and have it ready at a moment's notice. I had my saber out just as ZC-04 was about to strike. And he said that he was using a training saber, but man, that thing stung more than a regular training saber would. I also don't understand how the school could actually fire a teacher like Mr. Zefyr. Ugh! I can't believe I'm defending that guy. There are times when I can't stand him, which is pretty much all of the time, but we aren't supposed to be best friends with our teachers anyhow. I'm allowed to be annoyed and aggravated by him, yet totally angry that he was fired. Right?

Maybe not so bad?

We need to act now or I guarantee you, this all is going to get so much worse.

But what could we even do to stop ZC-04? He's stronger than all of us put together.

But truth is power, and if we could just get some intel on him, we may be able to take him down.

How would we even start to do that?

There must be something we could get from his office.

With all of the security droids patrolling the hallways? How would we even get anywhere near the front office?

83

You're sure this is going to work?!

Of course I'm not sure. But it's worth a try.

You have the right cable?

Yes. At least I hope I do. This should plug right into ZC-04's office computer, and I'll download all of the info onto my datapad.

86

Now, where were we . . .?

Um . . . we were looking to get a letter of recommendations for my apprenticeship application?

Sure thing. Just let me ask—what does Victor want in that office?

Triday

I guess my sweet Jedi skills are sharp because Mar didn't even acknowledge my presence when he walked in with ZC-04. I still can't believe I got out of there without getting caught. And that was a close call—my heart was beating in my stomach! It still is. I'm looking through all of this data that I swiped from ZC-04's computer. It's a lot to go through. I started by searching for info on P-10, RW-22, and T-3PO. They haven't been reprogrammed yet, but they're slated for tonight. They're in the student droid shop. I knew I should have signed up for that droid class. It would be so much easier for me to slip into the workshop and save them. Luckily, I know somebody who does . . . While I save our droids, Artemis is going to sift through the rest of the data.

So smart!

click

Bee-ba-BEE!

Oh, pal! I'm so happy to see you, too! Quick! Switch RW and T-3PO on, and we'll get you guys outta here!

Good heavens! What is the meaning of this?

BREEEEEE!

RW! Can you open this lock?

Somebody's coming?

step step

93

Vic! I uncovered some information, and it is not anything positive.

What's up?

It's Mr. Zefyr! He was fired by ZC-04 because he was critical of ZC-04's tactics. He was forming a movement among the faculty to remove ZC-04 from Jedi Academy!

ZC-04 finagled his way to become principal, so he could fire Mr. Zefyr!

That's twisted! We need to find Mr. Zefyr. He must know something that we don't.

Coruscant is a big planet, assuming he even stayed here. We'll never find him.

The statistical odds of you locating Mr. Zefyr are—

Beeow.

Find yourselves in the droid shop, do you? The meaning of this, you must tell me. Hmmm?

Quadday

I really can't know for sure what Yoda was trying to tell us. Did he want us to find Mr. Zefyr? Were we wrong in trying to liberate the droids? Should we just keep our heads low and survive the final days of Jedi Academy? On one hand, we could. But that would be the easiest thing to do. And I think what Yoda was trying to say is that sometimes the *right* thing to do can be the most *difficult* thing to do. We still had so much to learn from Zefyr. What if there were final lessons that would prove crucial to our future lives as Jedi? I just don't understand why Yoda doesn't fix all of this chaos. Couldn't he just track down Zefyr? Couldn't he just tell ZC-04 to chill?

If a Starspeeder brought all of this drama to Jedi Academy, I wanted to be the one to end it. But in order for me to do so, I needed to get some advice— from the smartest Starspeeder that I know.

What's up, Nerf Herder?

Chris, I need your help!

Make it quick, lil' bro, we're headed to Hoth. Reception is gonna get tricky.

I think I need to save the school!

Right. Vic, just study hard, don't talk back to Mr. Zefyr and you'll be—

That's just it! Zefyr was fired by that new security droid commander.

WHA?! How even?

And Yoda isn't doing anything about it!

And he told you that specifically? That he isn't doing anything?

No. But, I mean, I broke into the droid shop and—

VICTOR!

No, it was to save P-10 and the other droids. Yoda caught us, but didn't punish us.

Go on.

He said something about us just being Padawans, but Jedi must always make the right choice, no matter the difficulty. I'm paraphrasing, of course.

Paraphrasing, you are! Hmmmm?! He's testing you.

What?

I think Yoda is testing you. Hey, I gotta get going—

Dang! Lost connection.

VICTOR! Did you see this?!

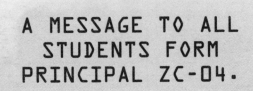

A MESSAGE TO ALL STUDENTS FORM PRINCIPAL ZC-04.

Effective immediately, the library at Jedi Academy will be closed. All texts will now flow directly to students via their datapads. All curricula that each instructor would like to teach must be approved by me personally before it can be disseminated to the student population. These measures are being taken so that we can assure parents that there are no Sith amongst the faculty who are looking to pollute the minds of young Padawans. It will also be against the new school policies for students to share information with their peers. No outside thought or instruction will be tolerated! Use of social media to criticize school policy is hereby forbidden on campus. Any students caught using social media for ill intent toward Jedi Academy will be immediately expelled.

Mr. Zefyr is still on Coruscant. But he's far.

106

But how are we even going to get one of these things moving. You have a key?

I haven't gotten that far yet.

Beee-ba-BEEEEEE!

Whoa! P-10! How did you get out?

Beee-beee-beeeeeee.

Yoda let you out?! See! That's a sign!

Bee-bee-BEOW!

Well then, P-10, get this ride started, and we'll be gone before they get here!

Before they get here?!

Monoday

I sure hope that Yoda is indeed testing me because we just sneaked off of campus. We also sort of borrowed an airspeeder. But I swear, we'll bring it back in mint condition. And it's school property, and weren't we at school to learn anyhow? I gave P-10 the coordinates for Mr. Zefyr's location, and he plugged them into the airspeeder's location system. I missed this ol' droid, and man, did he turn up just in time. It was also really helpful that P-10 put the airspeeder on autopilot mode. Flying simulators is one thing, but none of us had our licenses yet.

Elara has faith in me, but she was right—I definitely didn't plan out our escape properly. I also haven't planned out what we're going to say to Mr. Zefyr when we find him. I bet he'll just be so *thrilled* to see me. And he has to know that if *I* want him back at Jedi Academy, this has to be some serious business. And if Artemis is willing to break the rules, the stakes are definitely high. We need an adult's help, and Mr. Zefyr is the only hope!

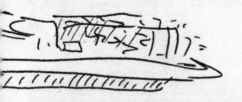

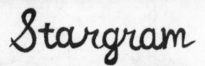

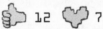 *MAYATHEATER:* Another day trying to decipher Wookiee stage direction.

 12 💚 7

 *Coletastic:* I think Kitmum wants us all to growl our way through the musical?

 5 💚 2

Duoday

Coruscant is even bigger than I expected it to be. When you attend Jedi Academy, you're sort of in your own little bubble—we rarely explore this city planet. With so much scum and villainy inhabiting the darker corners of this place, I can see why they'd want to keep us on campus. We'd been traveling nearly the entire day and I only sensed that we were about halfway to Mr. Zefyr. The traffic is just insane here. I don't know how anybody could live here with all of the city noises. Elara said that you get used to it and that when she visited me on Naboo, it was freaky to her how quiet it was there. I don't know—I don't think that I could deal with this city traffic, not when I know what a peaceful afternoon by the lake is like.

On the bright side, we're hungry and we found a great restaurant to stop in. They have hologames and everything! Elara said she went there a lot when she was a kid.

117

These three students went missing from Jedi Academy today. Hall monitors from the school will be sweeping the planet looking for them. If you see these three Padawans, please alert the nearest security droid. In other news . . .

I think we should get going.

EDITED BY THE STUDENTS OF JEDI ACADEMY Vol. MXVII #7

STUDENTS SPLIT SCHOOL!

Three Jedi Academy students have fled campus. Victor Starspeeder, Artemis Oophanoe, and Elara Ayres are wanted for questioning by Principal ZC-04. They were last spotted at a Spiffy's Space Port Arcade & Cantina location, 175 kilometers from the boundaries of Jedi Academy campus. While their current location is unknown, Principal ZC-04 is determined to bring them back to school to face the consequences of their actions. If any student has any knowledge as to why these students left or if anybody can pinpoint where they are heading, it is their moral obligation to do so. There will be no questions asked, and a handsome reward shall await. As a result of this insolence, students will no longer be allowed to participate in outdoor activities.

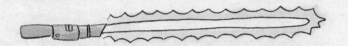

ASK MS. CATARA!

Dear Ms. Catara,

I hate watching my friend make decisions that land him in hot water. Even when his intentions are good, he gets tripped up and on the wrong side of the rules. But what if the rules are set up to make him fail? What if his actions are really the *right* thing to do? How do I support him? I hate getting in trouble myself, but what if I'm not doing enough to support my friend? I'm so conflicted.

Signed,
Conflicted

Dearza Conflicted,

Youza needs to know that you never will regret listening to youz gut. I'm not a talking about when youza hungry and youz tummy iza rumblin'. I mean listen to youz instincts. Numbah ones is to make sure youza and youz friend iza safe. Youza not goin' to change the worldz if youza not here tomorrow. So, if youz friend is making decisions that could put them in harm's way, tell a trusted adult rights awayz. But otherwize, stand tall next to youz friend if youza think it's the right thing to do.

XO,
Ms. Catara

COMICS

WOOKIEE CIRCUS

"RWOOOAR! RWAHHHH!"

SPOT THE DROIDRENCES!

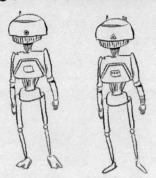

HUTTFIELD

YOUNGLINGS

GALAXY FEED

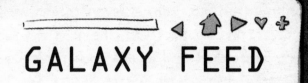

Most Intense
Hall Monitors
in the Galaxy

5 Creatures
to Lose Sleep
Over

The Best
Games at
Spiffy's Space
Port Arcade
& Cantina

Triday

We continued on our journey even though we didn't get a decent meal yet. I mean, the good news is that we weren't captured and hauled back to ZC-04. We stopped at a supply shop and grabbed a few quick snacks. Just something to tide us over, but I found myself missing the cafeteria food back at school. And that's saying something. It just didn't seem to be a good idea to stop and eat anywhere for too long. We had hall monitors on our trail, ready to haul us back to Jedi Academy and collect the reward. As much as my stomach wanted to eat . . .

I sensed that we were getting closer to Mr. Zefyr. Failure is not an option. If we don't find him and get sent back to school, we're all doomed. Yoda can't help as a teacher. We don't know if he's in on whatever is going on. We'll get kicked out of school and our futures will be in peril. None of us will get apprenticeships and we'll never be true Jedi. Just some has—beens who can levitate some junk.

I want to get Zefyr back so that I can pass his final exams and prove to him above all that I am a Padawan who is prepared for my time as a Jedi. When we find Zefyr and present him with the information that I swiped from ZC—04's office, he'll know just what to do with it to help us send ZC—04 packing.

Bee–be–BEE!

You're right! There it is. Mr. Zefyr is inside.

Mr. Zefyr works at Crazy Crio's Self-Defense Emporium?

I'm afraid so.

CRAZY CRIO'S SELF-DEFENSE Emporium

Here goes nothing . . .

Starspeeder, your road ends here.

WHOOOSH!

The security droids!

VWOOSH!

VWOOOSH!

Great work, P-10!

ZAP!

You all need to take this seriously if you expect to ward off intruders. Class dismissed.

Excuse me—

We're closed for the day. You can sign up for classes tomorrow.

We don't have that kind of time.

What are you kids doing here?!

We've come to bring you back to Jedi Academy.

I don't work there anymore.

Technically, you do.

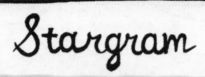

Stargram

MAYATHEATER: Bittersweet last show ever.

 12  7

Zav-YEAH: Still can't believe Victor is missing this.

 5 2

132

Coletastic: Showtime doesn't seem the same without all of our pals. #WhereisVictor?

👍 4   🤍 3

Emm-MET: I didn't expect to actually play the lead when I was cast as the understudy and now I am NERVOUS!

👍 7   🤍 11

We have all of the info we need to take you down, O'Halleran! Convenient that all of the security droids purchased by Jedi Academy were manufactured by your parents' company!

They're entrepreneurs. At least my parents aren't Sith!

Then what do you make of yourself then? You're not walking on the light side of the Force. You had your dad pull some strings and you got Principal Mar demoted. And then you banished Mr. Zefyr when he started catching on to your nonsense.

I haven't failed yet, Starspeeder.

It's over, Zach.

No. I set out to destroy this school . . .

And theret's one thing we have on our side that you don't, Zach . . .

The shadow of greed, jealousy is. From this stems all of this Padawan's problems, yes. Unfortunate, it is.

Go on, the show must! In tatters, the curtains are. Important, this is not.

Break a leg, Vic!

That's just the problem. I think I already did.

Emmett, go on. Take my place in the show.

But, Vic, you've always wanted the lead. And you've got that stage kiss ...

I already got a kiss. And it meant something.

Quadday

I always thought that I'd be the star of the show, but when showtime came, I was in no shape to sing and dance. Emmett was my understudy, and he did an incredible job with the part. He totally made it his own. Sure, I could have had that stage kiss with Maya, but that's just acting. I got a real kiss from Elara, and that meant so much more. It also meant so much to sit back and watch my friends put on an incredible show. They dedicated the performance to me, Elara, and Artemis. We legitimately saved the school! I mean, Yoda was never going to let anything really, really bad happen. But he gave me the greatest life lesson any Jedi needs to have to truly walk on the light side of the Force. The odds may seem unsurmountable, but you need to stand up and do what is right.

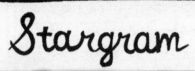

VICT-orious: This cast crushed their performance!

 12  7

VICT-orious: Standing ovation!

 15  22

No. When I see great potential, I push students to reach that potential.

May the Force be with you.

Students! Helmets fastened. Positions!

Engage hyperspace!

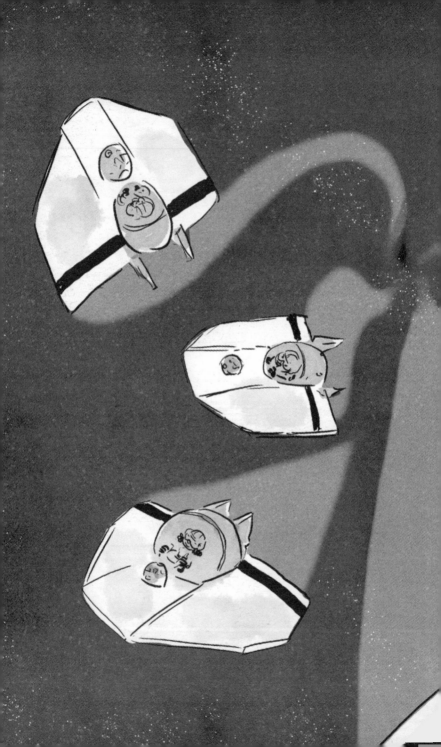

Pentaday

I ended up passing my final exam with Mr. Zefyr. I may not have gotten straight A's in all of my classes, but there are lots of different forms of intelligence. Artemis is really good at reading and memorizing facts, Elara has an emotional intelligence that is so insightful, and I have an intelligence with machinery and instincts, so sometimes my performances on tests don't truly reflect how smart I am. I keep getting complimented on my raw ability to use the Force. Yoda tells me that even though graduation is upon us, there is still much to learn. And I see what he means. The galaxy is vast and it has so much potential. If I get in with a good mentor, who knows what they'll be able to teach me. And I'll visit so many distant systems and worlds.

Wide open, the future is!

Student Name: Victor Starspeeder
Level: Padawan
Semester: Four

REPORT CARD

CLASS	NOTES	GRADES
JEDI MATH	Best of luck.	B
HISTORY OF THE JEDI ORDER	Thanks for saving the school. Could have worked harder in class...	C–
GALACTIC LITERATURE	It's been something...	B–
ADVANCED LIGHTSABER	Much improved	A
PHYSICAL EDUCATION FOR PADAWANS	*(handwritten scrawl)*	*(face doodle)*
METHODS IN PEACE NEGOTIATIONS	A true individual.	B
RECKONING WITH THE FORCE	Bright, the future is!	A

The Padawan Observer

DESPITE SETBACKS, STUDENTS FLOURISH

What a year for Jedi Academy students. It was an emotional roller coaster from start to finish! Thankfully, due to the work of hero students Victor Starspeeder, Elara Ayres, and Artemis Oophanoe, everyone will be headed into graduation just as they should be. All security droids have been scrapped, as has the early curfew.

The Padawan Observer End-of-Year Awards

Most Heroic

Brightest Star

Most Obsessed with Theater

Most Enthusiastic

Most Studious

Most Inspiring

Biggest Heart

Backward Most

Most Eager

Most Optimistic

Tallest

Beepiest

Stargram

VIC-torious: 2 J.A. alum in the Starspeeder fam!

 12   🤍 7

Elara-Force: I'm going to miss seeing this face every day!

👍 5   🤍 2

Coletastic: Yeah, that was my dad with the big sign in the audience.

👍 4 🤍 3

Zav-YEAH: We did it! #JediAcademyGrads

👍 7 🤍 11

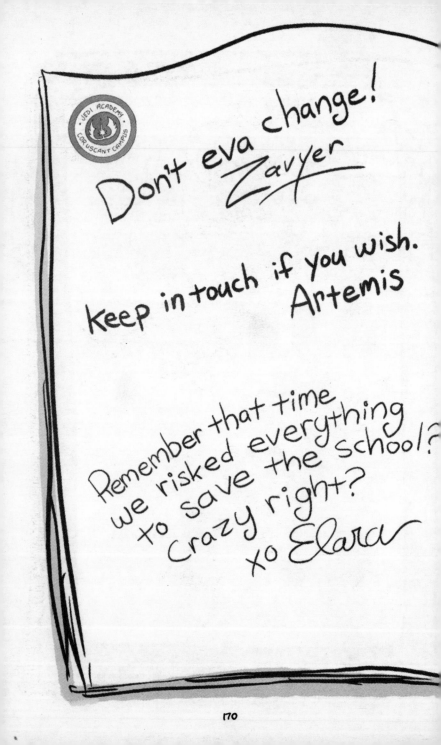

Great memories!
Emmett

You are _so_ talented!
Maya

You ROCK!
Coleman

A good summer you will have.
Yoda

JEDI ACADEMY · CORUSCANT CAMPUS

Heptaday

Now that I'm here, I'm not ready to say good-bye to Jedi Academy. But all good things must come to an end. But that has to happen in order for something else great to begin! And I'm set for my next adventure. I just received word that I will be studying under Tyn Jarsu, he's this crazy-cool Jedi who races across the galaxy in a custom-made starship. I think everything is going to be so awesome. I won't have my friends right with me every step of the way, but they'll just be a holocall away.

And we'll keep up with each other via Stargram, and we'll definitely get together when we have time off. I only wish P-10 could come.

I'm going to make everybody proud—Yoda, Mr. Zefyr —they'll see that all of their hard work and patience with me has paid off. Hey, maybe I'll even come back here and teach someday. That would be crazy, wouldn't it? Professor Starspeeder? HA!

Jarrett J. Krosoczka is a *New York Times* bestselling author, a two-time winner of the Children's Choice Book Award for the Third to Fourth Grade Book of the Year, an Eisner award nominee, and is the author and/or illustrator of more than thirty books for young readers. His work includes several picture books, the Lunch Lady graphic novels, and Platypus Police Squad middle-grade novel series. Jarrett has given two TED Talks, both of which have been curated to the main page of TED.com and have collectively accrued more than two million views online. He is also the host of The Book Report with JJK on SiriusXM's Kids Place Live, a weekly segment celebrating books, authors, and reading.

Jarrett lives in western Massachusetts with his wife and children, and their pugs, Ralph and Frank.